First World War
and Army of Occupation
War Diary
France, Belgium and Germany

33 DIVISION
Divisional Troops
Royal Army Medical Corps
99 and 101 Field Ambulance
and 33 Field Ambulance Workshop Unit
17 November 1915 - 31 March 1916

WO95/2418/2-5

The Naval & Military Press Ltd
www.nmarchive.com
Published in association with The National Archives

Published by

The Naval & Military Press Ltd

Unit 10 Ridgewood Industrial Park,

Uckfield, East Sussex,

TN22 5QE England

Tel: +44 (0) 1825 749494

www.naval-military-press.com

www.nmarchive.com

This diary has been reprinted in facsimile from the original. Any imperfections are inevitably reproduced and the quality may fall short of modern type and cartographic standards.

© Crown Copyright
Images reproduced by permission of The National Archives, London, England, 2015.

Contents

Document type	Place/Title	Date From	Date To
Heading	WO95/2418-4 33 Field Amb Workshop Nov 1915-Mar 1916		
Heading	33rd Division Medical 33rd Fd Amb Workshop Unit. Nov 1915-March 1916		
Heading	33rd F.A.W.U. Vol I 1218/7935 Nov 1915		
Heading	War Diary. Of 33rd F.A.W.U. Officer Commanding		
War Diary	Southampton	17/11/1915	17/11/1915
War Diary	Haure	18/11/1915	18/11/1915
War Diary	Roven	19/11/1915	21/11/1915
War Diary	Infatal	21/11/1915	22/11/1915
War Diary	Hesdin	22/11/1915	22/11/1915
War Diary	Hinbegice	23/11/1915	23/11/1915
War Diary	Bussus	24/11/1915	29/11/1915
War Diary	Auneyin	30/11/1915	30/11/1915
Heading	Dec 1915		
War Diary	Auneyin	01/12/1915	31/12/1915
Heading	F Jan 1916		
War Diary	Auneyin	01/01/1916	31/01/1916
Heading	Feb 1916		
War Diary	Auneyin	01/02/1916	29/02/1916
Heading	War Diary of 33rd Divisional Field Ambulance Workshop Unit For March 1916		
War Diary	Auneyin Les Bethune	01/03/1916	31/03/1916

WO 95/2418/4

33 FIELD AMB WORKSHOP NOV 1915 - MAR 1916

33RD DIVISION
MEDICAL

33RD FD AMB WORKSHOP UNIT.
NOV 1915-MARCH 1916

33RD DIVISION
MEDICAL

33rd R.A.W.U.
Vol I

12/7935

Nov 1915

November 1915

Yours sincerely,

A.

33rd F.A.W.U.
Officer Commanding

P Sangster
2 Lieut A.S.C.

Army Form C. 2118.

WAR DIARY
or
INTELLIGENCE SUMMARY
(Erase heading not required.)

Instructions regarding War Diaries and Intelligence Summaries are contained in F. S. Regs., Part II and the Staff Manual respectively. Title pages will be prepared in manuscript.

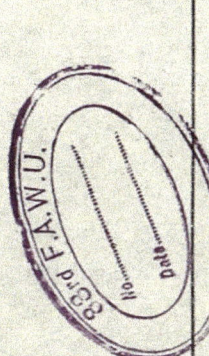
83rd F.A.W.U.

Place	Date	Hour	Summary of Events and Information	Remarks and references to Appendices
	1916			
Southampton	Nov 17		Sailed from Southampton with 531 men. Vehicle convoy having already sailed for Havre movement.	
Havre	18th		Arrived Havre 2 AM. Spent day at Rest Camp. Horse Boarded Train for Rouen 8 PM.	
Rouen	19th		Arrived Rouen 7 PM. Picked up convoy and billeted in Rest Camp. Stour state	
	20th		Rest Camp Rouen. Sent two men to hospital 1 Venereal & 1 Hand case. Stores declared store	
	21st		Inspection of men and vehicles 11 AM. Proceeded in convoy to Nortalettet 1/30 arrived	
Nortalettet	"		Nortalettet 6/10 PM. Rested overnight.	
	22		Proceeded in convoy 9 AM reported Abbiville Road at S Remaltel Gravel. Received instructions to	
	"		proceed Hesdin en route for Aubigne made Hesdin 8 PM Rested	
Hesdin	"		Inspect vehicles & mounted guard.	
Hesdin area	23		Proceeded Aubigne 10 AM arrived 3 PM. 33rd Division had moved off,	
	"		after much searching found Supply Col. Lent them left in Havehook to	
	"		find one Parked and mounted guard on cars to R Penard Park 4 AM.	
Burnia	24.		Reported A.D.M.S. 33rd Division Halted mer Aubiquie Proceed Fuckel and Marche	
			to Poulk of Gravel	

WAR DIARY
INTELLIGENCE SUMMARY
(Erase heading not required.)

Army Form C. 2118.

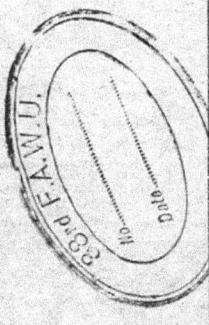

Place	Date	Hour	Summary of Events and Information	Remarks and references to Appendices
Buones	1915 25.		Rafaled ADMS. Proceeded D.D.o.S. 1st Army to report and obtain information as to evacuation of vehicles beyond the repairing power of my workshop.	
Buones	26.		I.O. van reports arrived out in Workshop. Towed damaged Ambulance No. 19517 to G.H.Q. (Steffield Gears) for replacement.	
Buones	27.		Workshop routine well in hand and no more spare ambulance with my workshop staff. Seven Ambulances and 1 Mot. Car attacks to 700th Brigade transferred to 2nd April 2 cars in place to 1 Ambulance at 3 M. Gun. 1st to 97th Brigade 35th division.	
Buones	28.		Workshop arriving Hackney Ford 7am to 2/30 PM on 30 HP Fairbanks attached Tenter and Motor Tender. SUGGESTION 2 cornes that Public cars able to a 10HP Dodge will be to means available at about half the cost	

WAR DIARY
or
INTELLIGENCE SUMMARY

(Erase heading not required.)

Army Form C. 2118.

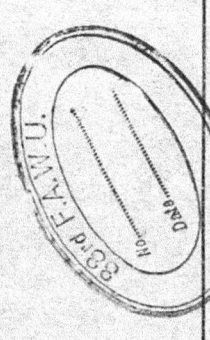

Place	Date	Hour	Summary of Events and Information	Remarks and references to Appendices
Burnt	Nov 1915 29th		Tpr. J. Perkins "B" Sqn diary created during the night and to first in aid of troops a full sergeant of Aus. Troop & engine of Bulawar and have ten h.p. male bonnet which was covered with sacks as a water precaution. I am unable to it once sun counted all wound fires. Deserts of the means for replacement against front effects. Report and Parless tops without aim flashes and portion of rugine maked top.	
Ameryin	30th		Arranged blink as Parts for Turkish G.T.S. Spares &c. Ammyin a 9 horse vehicle this a 9 steated vin.	

33rd F.A. w.v.
Vol: 2

U.S.F.

Dec 1915

WAR DIARY
or
INTELLIGENCE SUMMARY.
(Erase heading not required.)

Army Form C. 2118.

Instructions regarding War Diaries and Intelligence Summaries are contained in F. S. Regs., Part II. and the Staff Manual respectively. Title pages will be prepared in manuscript.

Place	Date	Hour	Summary of Events and Information	Remarks and references to Appendices
Rouen	December 1st 1915		Completed erection of shelters over workshop stands. Ambulance for 99th Field Ambulance in with stripped gears. (17506)	
	2nd		Carried out running repairs. Robert for store. Repaired Workshop and Stores routine	
	3rd		Workshop routine	
	4th		Daimler Ambulance 17506 car maker to G.H.Q. Officer over recovered very badly	
	5th		Fixed up Officers car. At request of A.D.M.S. went to inspect a stores lorry for Divisional Laundry Purposes at Ellers	
	6th		Proceeded Ellers to A.D.M.S. re lorry for Laundry purposes. Clearing up of workshop yard	
	7th		Set out to Ellers to demand Laundry lorry & ambulance for transport to Boitaine. Workshop routine	

Army Form C. 2118.

WAR DIARY
or
INTELLIGENCE SUMMARY.
(Erase heading not required.)

Instructions regarding War Diaries and Intelligence Summaries are contained in F. S. Regs., Part II. and the Staff Manual respectively. Title pages will be prepared in manuscript.

Place	Date	Hour	Summary of Events and Information	Remarks and references to Appendices
Amiens	February 1915			
	8th		Worked on usual Bibs. Various Workshops Routine.	
	9th		Officers car taken for use of 188 Coy Special RE unit authority from D.S.T.	
	10th		Both cycle Triumph in note sister frame	
	11th		Received replacement for Launces Ambulance evacuated on 4th inst.	
	12th		Launces No 1738. Ambulance in collision with lorry J to 2372. Secondary section. Passed into Workshops	
	13th		Passed Launce No 1754 Ambulance to G.H.Q. Received replacement for same No 1751, evacuated to G.H.Q. on 28th Feb 1915. Evacuated Triumph M 8400 to 33 Coy Supply Col. Indented for motor cycle to make up.	
	14th		Nothing when stated.	

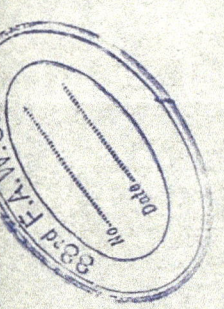

WAR DIARY or INTELLIGENCE SUMMARY

Army Form C. 2118.

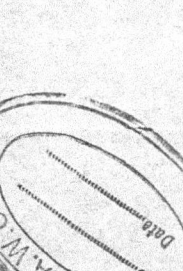

Place	Date	Hour	Summary of Events and Information	Remarks and references to Appendices
Amenyin	December 1915			
	15th		Inspected 101st Field Ambulance vehicles.	
	16th		Evacuated Samba Ambulance 496 with the usual complaint of stripped gears.	
	17th		Inspected Ambulances vehicles of the 19th F.A. and 99 F	
	18th		Proceeded Sonkim for the inspection of 99th F.A. Purchased new axle steel for blacksmith.	
	19th		Workshop routine	
	20th		Attended court of enquiry re accident to Lambes 17311 in 12th and Explanation sent to DDST re accounts of Lambes mentioned in the diary (3 stripped gears 1 bearing)	
	21st		Proceeded Killis met Capt Heyworth ASC to inspect another lorry and the CB for steam lorry 16 men at Amenyin found CB light not in charge of evection. Wrote and	
	22nd		...	

Army Form C. 2118.

WAR DIARY
or
INTELLIGENCE SUMMARY.
(Erase heading not required.)

Instructions regarding War Diaries and Intelligence Summaries are contained in F. S. Regs., Part II. and the Staff Manual respectively. Title pages will be prepared in manuscript.

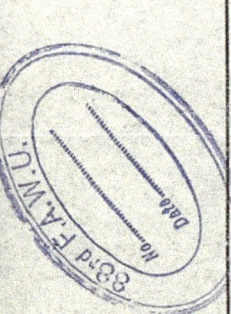

Place	Date	Hour	Summary of Events and Information	Remarks and references to Appendices
Chevigny	23rd		Proceeded on Laundry Bale & Tanks. Truck reported to General Benson as expected.	
	24"		As for 23rd	
	25"		(Sunday 25) Xmas Day	
	26th		As for 23rd	
	27"		As for 23rd. Sunday shg. 26 norms.	
	28th		As for 23rd. Proceeded to Chino to inspect pipes into fire at Ford Aérodrome arrived & took fire at No 1 Shed, Shed, little damage killed.	
	29"		As for 23rd	
	30"		As for 23rd	
	31		Proceeded Hazebrouck to inspect boiler with Capt Heynworth A.S.C. Boiler N.G. not	

33rd F.a.w.u.
vol: 3

F

Jun 1916

WAR DIARY
or
INTELLIGENCE SUMMARY.
(Erase heading not required.)

Army Form C. 2118.

O.C. 33RD DIV.F.A.W.U.
LIEUT. A.S.C.

Place	Date	Hour	Summary of Events and Information	Remarks and references to Appendices
Amiens	Feby 1st 1916	1.	Proceeded No 1 Harly St to recover remains of Ford Ambulance destroyed by shell fire on 28th Dec. 1915	
		2.	Supervised Laundry & workshop	
		3.	Returned. ordered to return to Base. Returned completion of Laundry work to 2y General Tender cd.	
		4.	Three Ambulances and 1 motor cycle in workshop for repair	
		5.	Workshop routine	
		6.	Workshop routine	
		7.	Workshop routine	
		8.	Workshop routine	
		9.	Workshop routine	
		10.	Workshop routine. Car returned from 186 Special R.E. Coy	
		11.	Workshop routine	

Army Form C. 2118.

WAR DIARY
or
INTELLIGENCE SUMMARY.
(Erase heading not required.)

Instructions regarding War Diaries and Intelligence Summaries are contained in F. S. Regs., Part II. and the Staff Manual respectively. Title pages will be prepared in manuscript.

Place	Date	Hour	Summary of Events and Information	Remarks and references to Appendices
Auvigny	January 1916. 12.		Workshop routine. Fairly took disposed from G.H.Q. Works.	
	13.		Workshop routine	
	14.		Workshop routine	
	15.		Received Petrol & Gas Cylinders in place of First Ambulance destroyed by shell fire on 28th December 1915.	
	16.		Workshop routine	
	17.		Workshop routine	
	18.		Workshop routine	
	19.		Workshop routine	
	20.		Workshop routine	
	21.		Workshop routine	
	22.		Workshop routine	
	23.		Workshop routine	

O.C. 33RD DIV. F.A.W.U.
LIEUT. A.S.C.

Army Form C. 2118.

WAR DIARY
or
INTELLIGENCE SUMMARY.
(Erase heading not required.)

Instructions regarding War Diaries and Intelligence Summaries are contained in F. S. Regs., Part II. and the Staff Manual respectively. Title pages will be prepared in manuscript.

Place	Date	Hour	Summary of Events and Information	Remarks and references to Appendices
Aumey	January 1916			
	24		Workshops routine	
	25		Workshops routine	
	26		Workshops routine	
	27		Workshops routine	
	28		Workshops routine	
	29		Workshops routine	
	30		Workshops routine	
	31		Workshops routine	

M Bendy
LIEUT. A.S.C.
O.C. 33RD DIV. F.A.W.U.

33
F.A.W.O. / Vol. 4

Feb. 1916

Army Form C. 2118

WAR DIARY
or
INTELLIGENCE SUMMARY
(Erase heading not required.)

Instructions regarding War Diaries and Intelligence Summaries are contained in F.S. Regs., Part II. and the Staff Manual respectively. Title Pages will be prepared in manuscript.

Place	Date	Hour	Summary of Events and Information	Remarks and references to Appendices
Amiens	FEB 1st 1916 to 10th		Ordinary Motor Ambulance Workshops Routine.	
"	11th		Workshops Routine and Inspection of Foden Steam Lorry.	
"	12th		Proceeded Bray to A.D.M.S. to inspect Motor Ambulance tents arrangement	
"	13th		Designed improved form of tent apparatus. Workshops Routine and Inspection of Ambulances.	
"	15th to 21st		Ordinary Motor Ambulance Workshops Routine. 21st Feb Inspection of Motor Ambulances Foden Lorry and Cycle apparatus	
"	not 15 22nd to 24th		Workshops Routine.	
"	25th		Completed aught experimental model of tent apparatus for motor ambulances.	
"	26th to 29th		Workshops Routine.	

[signature] LIEUT. A.S.C.
O.C. 33RD. DIV. F.A.W.U.

33rd F.A.W.U.
No.—
Date 2/2/16

WAR DIARY

of

33rd Divisional Field Ambulance Workshop Unit

For March 1916

COMMITTEE FOR THE
MEDICAL HISTORY OF THE W

Date

33D⁰ FAWU

Army Form C. 2118

WAR DIARY
or
INTELLIGENCE SUMMARY
(Erase heading not required.)

Vol 6

33rd F.A.W.U.
Registered
Date: August 1916

O.C. 33rd Div. F.A.W.U.
Lieut. A.S.C.

Place	Date	Hour	Summary of Events and Information	Remarks and references to Appendices
Auxey-les-Bethune	March 1st		Workshop routine. Rected French stretcher carrier for A.D.M.S.	
	2nd		Two ambulance motors in for repairs.	
	3rd		Three ambulance motors in for repairs.	
	4th		New stretch trolley started. Workshop routine.	
	5th		Tested stretcher truck at Lenbrin.	
	6th		Two cars in for repair. Tested motor cycle and 1 car in for repairs.	
	7th		Two motor cycles and 1 car and 1 car completed.	
	8th		Repairs to motor cycle 1 and workshop duty. Routine attentions to workshop and plant.	
	9th		do. do. Routine special operating stretcher for D.M.S.	
	10th & 12th		Ruling routine. Completed operating stretcher and repaired stretcher truck.	
	12th, 13th, 14th, 15th		Completed alternative drive to workshop. Truck attention to disposition of workshop vehicles, for general workshop efficiency.	

Army Form C. 2118

WAR DIARY
or
INTELLIGENCE SUMMARY
(Erase heading not required.)

Instructions regarding War Diaries and Intelligence Summaries are contained in F.S. Regs, Part II. and the Staff Manual respectively. Title Pages will be prepared in manuscript.

88th F.A.W.U.
No. ......
Date ......

Place	Date	Hour	Summary of Events and Information	Remarks and references to Appendices
Annezin lez Bethune	March 8th 1916			
	20th–25th		Started on special stretcher truck No. 2. 1 car in for repairs. Alterations to special Daimler ambulance heating apparatus. Delivery workshop routine.	
	25th – 30th		Relieving workshop repairs and routine.	
	31st		Under G.R.O. 1484 dated 30-3-16 this unit ceases to exist &c. Amalgamated with the 33rd Division Supply Column.	

P. Beaufort
LIEUT. A.S.C.
O.C. 33RD DIV. F.A.W.